Level 5

MATHS
Workbook

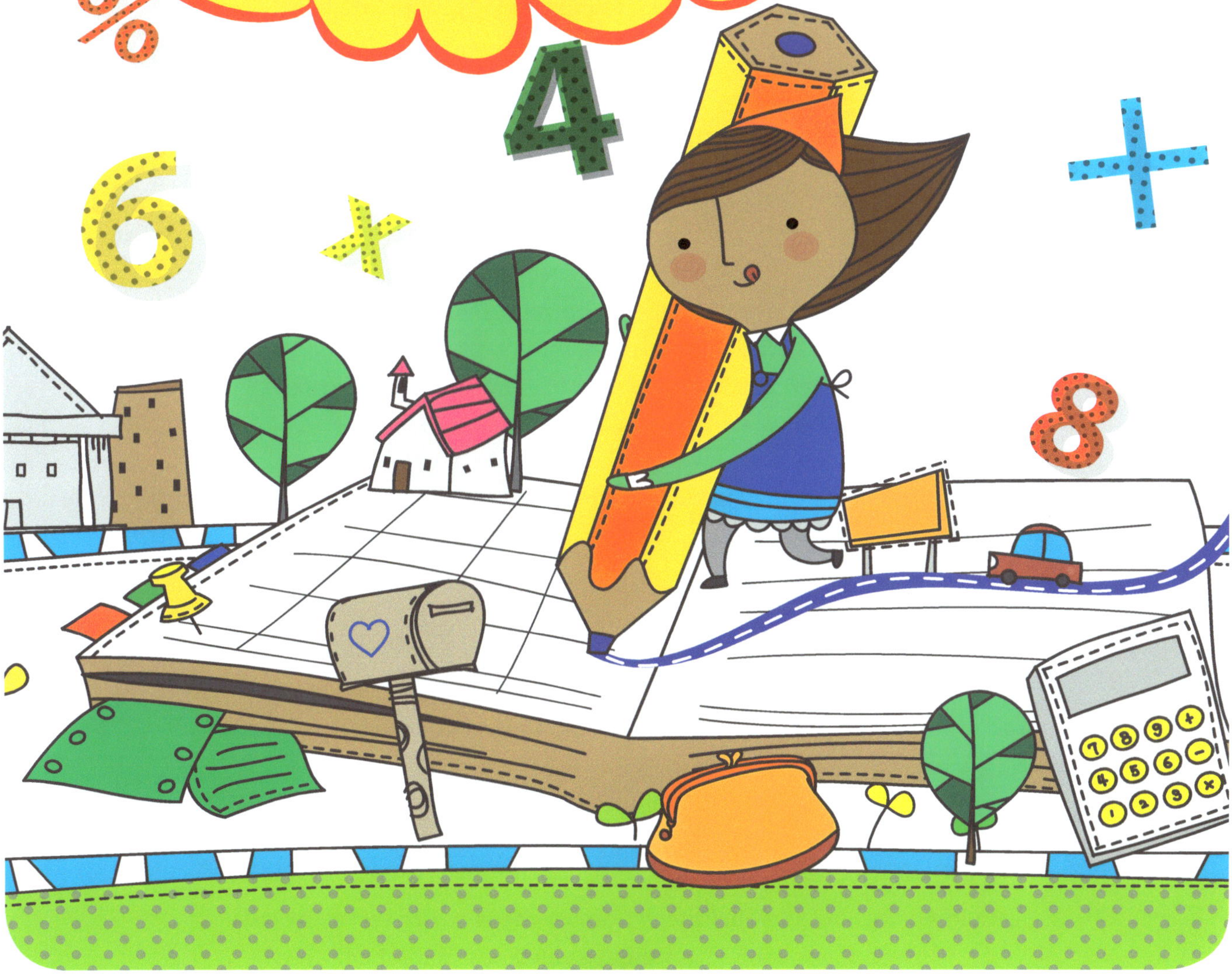

MOONSTONE

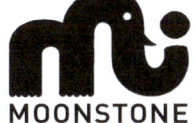

Published in Moonstone
by Rupa Publications India Pvt. Ltd 2022
7/16, Ansari Road, Daryaganj
New Delhi 110002

Sales centres:
Allahabad Bengaluru Chennai
Hyderabad Jaipur Kathmandu
Kolkata Mumbai

Copyright © Rupa Publications India Pvt. Ltd 2022

The views and opinions expressed in this book are
the authors' own and the facts are as reported by them
which have been verified to the extent possible,
and the publishers are not in any way liable for the same.

All rights reserved.
No part of this publication may be reproduced, transmitted,
or stored in a retrieval system, in any form or by any means,
electronic, mechanical, photocopying, recording or otherwise,
without the prior permission of the publisher.

ISBN: 978-93-5520-716-6

First impression 2022

10 9 8 7 6 5 4 3 2 1

The moral right of the authors has been asserted.

Printed in India
This book is sold subject to the condition that it shall not,
by way of trade or otherwise, be lent, resold, hired out, or otherwise
circulated, without the publisher's prior consent, in any form of binding
or cover other than that in which it is published.

Contents

Large Numbers...4

Arithmetic Operations...10

Factors and Multiples...16

Fractions..20

Decimals..25

Patterns and Symmetry..29

Geometry...33

Perimeter...41

Metric Measurements...43

Answers...46

Large Numbers

1. Write the following numbers in the given place value chart.

   (a) 4678785
   (b) 988776543
   (c) 20085300
   (d) 15608754
   (e) 13469902
   (f) 2534708

Crores		Lakhs		Thousands		Ones		
TC	C	TL	L	TTh	Th	H	T	O

2. Write the number name for each of the following.

   a. 38,42,950 = _____

   b. 1,04,36,008 = _____

   c. 86,54,037 = _____

   d. 2,59,80,856 = _____

   e. 7,04,13,806 = _____

3. **Find the sum of the place values of the underlined digits.**

   (a) 4<u>2</u>30<u>7</u>89 _____

   (b) 65<u>8</u>356<u>8</u> _____

   (c) <u>1</u>86400<u>2</u>8 _____

   (d) 8<u>3</u>70<u>2</u>084 _____

4. **Find the difference of the place values of the underlined digits.**

   (a) <u>7</u>40<u>8</u>432 _____

   (b) <u>3</u>847<u>2</u>008 _____

   (c) 12<u>9</u>0083<u>2</u> _____

   (d) 16<u>5</u>8765<u>0</u> _____

5. **Write the following numbers in the standard form.**

   a. Sixty lakh four thousand seven hundred thirteen _____

   b. Three crore seventy five lakh eight hundred one _____

   c. 2000000 + 60000 + 4000 + 500 + 60 + 9 _____

   d. 10000000 + 800000 + 50000 + 3000 + 80 + 7 _____

   e. Fifteen lakh twenty nine thousand nine hundred twenty _____

6. **Write the following numbers in the expanded form.**

   a. 3,49,08,462 _____

   b. 50,08,20,067 _____

   c. 2,79,84,600 _____

   d. 86,08,059 _____

   e. 7,36,40,708 _____

7. **Complete the table given below.**

	Predecessor	Number	Successor
a.		3,29,189	
b.		76,99,999	
c.		5,00,00,000	
d.		36,29,080	
e.		72,46,89,999	

8. **Compare the following numbers using >, < or =.**

a. 39,78,462 ☐ 3,79,48,625   b. 25,99,008 ☐ 25,99,008

c. 1,25,78,004 ☐ 1,26,78,004   d. 73,64,296 ☐ 3,07,59,878

e. 46,37,082 ☐ 63,47,820   f. 3,70,14,880 ☐ 3,71,04,800

g. 1,64,78,390 ☐ 1,46,87,093   h. 8,64,00,380 ☐ 8,64,83,000

9. **Form the greatest and smallest numbers using the given digits only once.**

	Digits	Greatest Number	Smallest Number
a.	3, 8, 0, 4, 1, 3, 8		
b.	7, 5, 3, 2, 8, 0, 9, 2		
c.	1, 9, 5, 4, 8, 7, 6, 3		
d.	0, 8, 7, 6, 6, 2, 4, 9		
e.	2, 0, 1, 9, 7, 5, 3, 8		
f.	1, 7, 4, 2, 0, 1, 0, 8		

10. Arrange the following in the ascending order.

a. 3642897, 3824926, 3682497, 3256728, 3392647

_____

b. 60198527, 61098572, 69084217, 60052947, 65284272

_____

11. Arrange the following in the descending order.

a. 8427650, 8475600, 8465270, 8472650, 8472560

_____

b. 14297600, 14286700, 14892700, 14209670, 14205267

_____

12. Fill in the blanks with the correct numbers.

a. The sum of the greatest and the smallest 8-digit number is _____.

b. 1 less than the smallest 7-digit number is _____.

c. The difference of the smallest 5-digit number and the greatest 7-digit number is _____.

d. Five times the smallest 8-digit number is _____.

e. The sum of the smallest 7-digit number and the greatest 6-digit number is _____.

f. 1 less than the greatest 8-digit number is _____.

g. 1 more than the smallest 5-digit number is _____.

h. 1 more than the largest 7-digit number is _____.

13. Round of the following numbers to the nearest 1000.

a. 6,74,285 _____   b. 75,00,800 _____

c. 28,93,651 _____   d. 16,42,147 _____

e. 28,69,499 _____   f. 2,37,00,525 _____

14. Round off the following numbers to the nearest 100.

a. 18,84,065 _____   b. 37,64,550 _____

c. 80,04,349 _____   d. 6,79,984 _____

e. 25,07,925 _____   f. 2,64,508 _____

15. Round off the following numbers to the nearest 10,000.

a. 29,78,564 _____   b. 6,19,35,200 _____

c. 64,70,925 _____   d. 29,98,567 _____

e. 23,28,716 _____   f. 71,50,800 _____

16. Round off the following numbers to the nearest 1000 and then write their number names.

a. 6,42,738 = _____

b. 3,04,290 = _____

c. 82,997 = _____

d. 6,14,529 = _____

17. Write the Hindu-Arabic numerals for the following Roman numerals.

a. LXXV _____   b. CCII _____

c. MDLV _____   d. MCCXII _____

e. CMLXV _____   f. CXIX _____

g. CLVII _____   h. DXXXVIII _____

i. MMLIV _____

18. Write the Roman numerals for the following Hindu-Arabic numerals.

a. 1720 _____   b. 800 _____

c. 2017 _____   d. 568 _____

e. 1110 _____   f. 253 _____

g. 947 _____   h. 404 _____

i. 1616 _____

19. Answer the following using Roman numerals.

a. The year in which you were born _____.

b. The number of days in a leap year _____.

c. There are _____ minutes in 12 hours.

d. There are _____ letters in the English alphabet.

e. The greatest 3-digit number is _____.

f. The smallest 4-digit number is _____.

g. The fifteenth multiple of 9 is _____.

h. The first five prime numbers are _____, _____, _____, _____ and _____.

i. The next year is _____.

j. The successor of 597 is _____.

k. The predecessor of 1000 is _____.

Arithmetic Operations

1. **Solve the following and mark the periods.**

   (a)   7 3 2 0 8 9
       + 1 6 7 2 4 3
       _____

   (b)   2 0 0 8 4 9 7
       +   8 8 2 6 0 5
       _____

   (c)   5 0 2 0 6 4 3
       +   9 3 5 8 0 7
       _____

   (d)   4 3 9 2 7 6
       − 2 4 0 8 4 3
       _____

   (e)   8 0 0 0 2 9 3
       −   3 2 1 4 9 7
       _____

   (f)   6 7 2 8 4 1
       − 1 5 7 3 6 0
       _____

2. **Write the missing digits in the following problems.**

   (a)
2	3	4		8
+		9	2	0	8
7	7		1	7

   (b)
8		0	7	0		8
−			2	6		0
4	7		2	3	0	3

3. **Answer the following problems.**

   a. 623597 more than 2164239 is _____

   b. 3264900 more than 2842968 is _____

   c. 4804204 less than 10000000 is _____

   d. 999999 less than 1000000 is _____

   e. Subtract 297643 from 8629941 _____

   f. Add 863942 and 642709 _____

   g. 6873498 less than 9090909 is _____

   h. 255682 more than 5738065 is _____

4. **Read the problems and find the solution.**

a. The sum of 6,43,882 and 1,34,525 is subtracted from 8,00,000. Find the difference obtained. _____

b. A company manufactured 83,40,000 products in a year out of which only 43,76,528 were sold. How many products were left unsold? _____

c. Manav had $62,73,500 in his bank account. He paid two bills worth $3,89,200 and $46,500 respectively. How much money is left in his bank account after making the payments? _____

d. The farmers of a village produced 78,64,390 kg of grains in a year. They kept 43,270 kg for their household use and sold the rest. What amount of grain was sold by the farmers? _____

5. **Follow the directions and complete the number chain.**

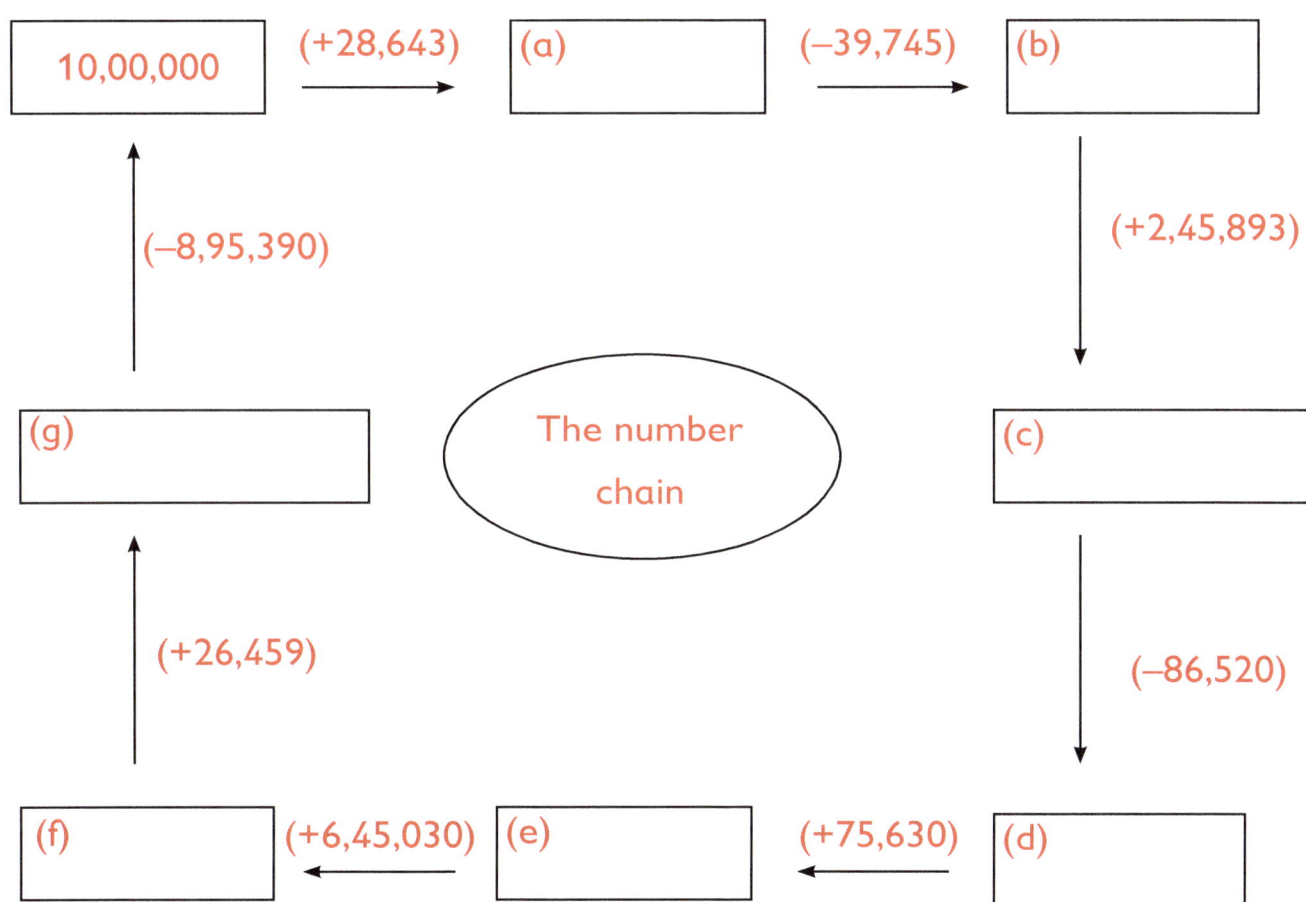

6. Arrange in columns and solve.

a. 462875 × 28

b. 308977 × 16

c. 39528 ÷ 12

d. 286400 ÷ 4

7. Answer the following problems mentally.

a. 6428 × 100 = _____

b. 32050 × 1000 = _____

c. 15268 × 10 = _____

d. 452670 × 8 = _____

e. _____ × 400 = 240000

f. 700 × _____ = 630000

g. 6729000 ÷ 100 = _____

h. 4685080 ÷ _____ = 468508

i. 2376500 ÷ 10 = _____

j. 8426000 ÷ 1000 = _____

8. **Answer the following word problems.**

a. A factory produces 36,498 toys everyday. Find the number of toys produced in the month of January. _____

b. 78,29,640 stamps are to be distributed equally between 14 post offices. Find out the number of stamps that will be received by each post office. Also find out the number of stamps left (if any). _____, _____

c. Shruti reads 245 pages daily. Calculate how many pages she can read in a leap year. _____

d. 16,43,250 people travelled through ship in a year. If equal number of people were carried by each ship and 25 ship rides were conducted, how many people can travel in one ride? _____

9. **Complete the given operations to find the solution.**

a.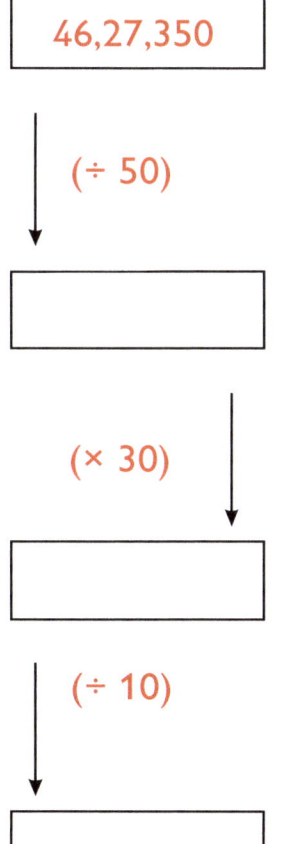

b.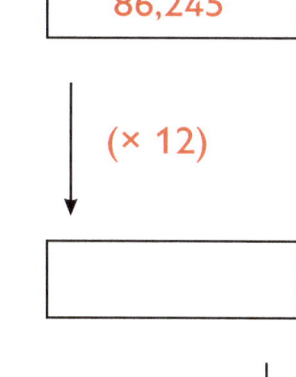

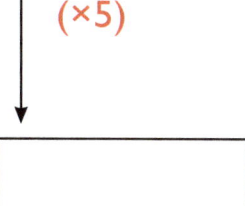

10. Find the answers to the sums and write the round off figures.

a. 1,86,429 + 2,45,397	b. 8,29,786 − 3,78,465	c. 6,42,908 ÷ 11
d. 38,429 × 22	e. 6,84,792 × 8	

11. Estimate the answer for the following and compare it with the actual answer.

a. A tree can grow 64,82,976 leaves in a year. Estimate the number of leaves that grow in a month.

b. Max collected 39,826 stamps in a year. He gifted 4829 of them to his younger brother. How many stamps are left with him now?

c. 17,826 cartons are used to transport books from one place to another. If each carton contains 536 books, how many books are there in all?

12. Fill in the blanks.

a. The sum of the greatest 6-digit number and the smallest 7-digit number is _____.

b. The difference of the smallest 8-digit number and the largest 7-digit number is _____.

c. The product of the greatest 4-digit number and the smallest 4-digit number is _____.

d. The quotient obtained after dividing the smallest 8-digit number by the smallest 4-digit number is _____.

e. The product of the greatest 6-digit number and 0 is _____.

f. The product of the smallest 3-digit number and 567 is _____.

g. The quotient obtained after dividing 66766 by the greatest 2-digit number is _____ and the remainder is _____.

13. Write the missing digits for the following.

a. ☐99☐88 × 100 = 99988800

b. 121000 ÷ ☐2☐ = 1000

c. 3☐4102☐ × 2 = 6682048

d. 462☐8 + 10000 = 56248

e. 6666000 ÷ ☐6 = 101000

f. 2020202 + ☐0☐0☐0 = 2323232

g. 6842908 − 3☐20☐0☐ = 3322000

Factors and Multiples

1. **Fill in the blanks.**

a. _____ is neither prime nor a composite number.

b. The _____ of a number are either less than or equal to the number.

c. The _____ of a number are either more than or equal to the number.

d. Prime numbers have only _____ factors.

e. _____ numbers have more than two factors.

f. The product of two numbers is always equal to the product of their _____ and _____.

g. HCF means _____ and LCM means _____.

h. Two prime numbers which differ by 2 are called _____.

2. **Write all the factors of the given numbers.**

a. 32 _____   b. 15 _____

c. 40 _____   d. 28 _____

e. 66 _____   f. 14 _____

3. **Write the first three multiples of the following numbers.**

a. 8 _____   b. 15 _____

c. 5 _____   d. 10 _____

e. 22 _____   f. 11 _____

4. Write all the prime numbers between 20 and 60.

_____

5. Write all the twin primes between 1 and 100.

_____

6. Find the prime factorization of the following numbers using the factor tree method.

a. 72

b. 150

c. 176

d. 108

7. Find the LCM of the following numbers by listing their multiples.

a. 2, 3 and 7.

b. 4, 6 and 12.

8. Answer the following questions.

a. The product of two numbers is 750 and their HCF is 5. Find their LCM. _____

b. Find the number which can divide both the numbers 450 and 315 exactly without leaving any remainder. _____

c. The product of LCM and HCF of two numbers is 184. If one of the numbers is 8, find the other number. _____

d. Find the HCF and LCM of the numbers 15 and 27. _____

e. Find the LCM of the numbers 55 and 77 if their HCF is 11. _____

f. Find the largest number that divides 96 and 108 without leaving any remainder. _____

9. **Myra wants to draw a rectangle of area 48 square units. Find the factors of 48 and draw all possible rectangles of area 48 square units for her.**

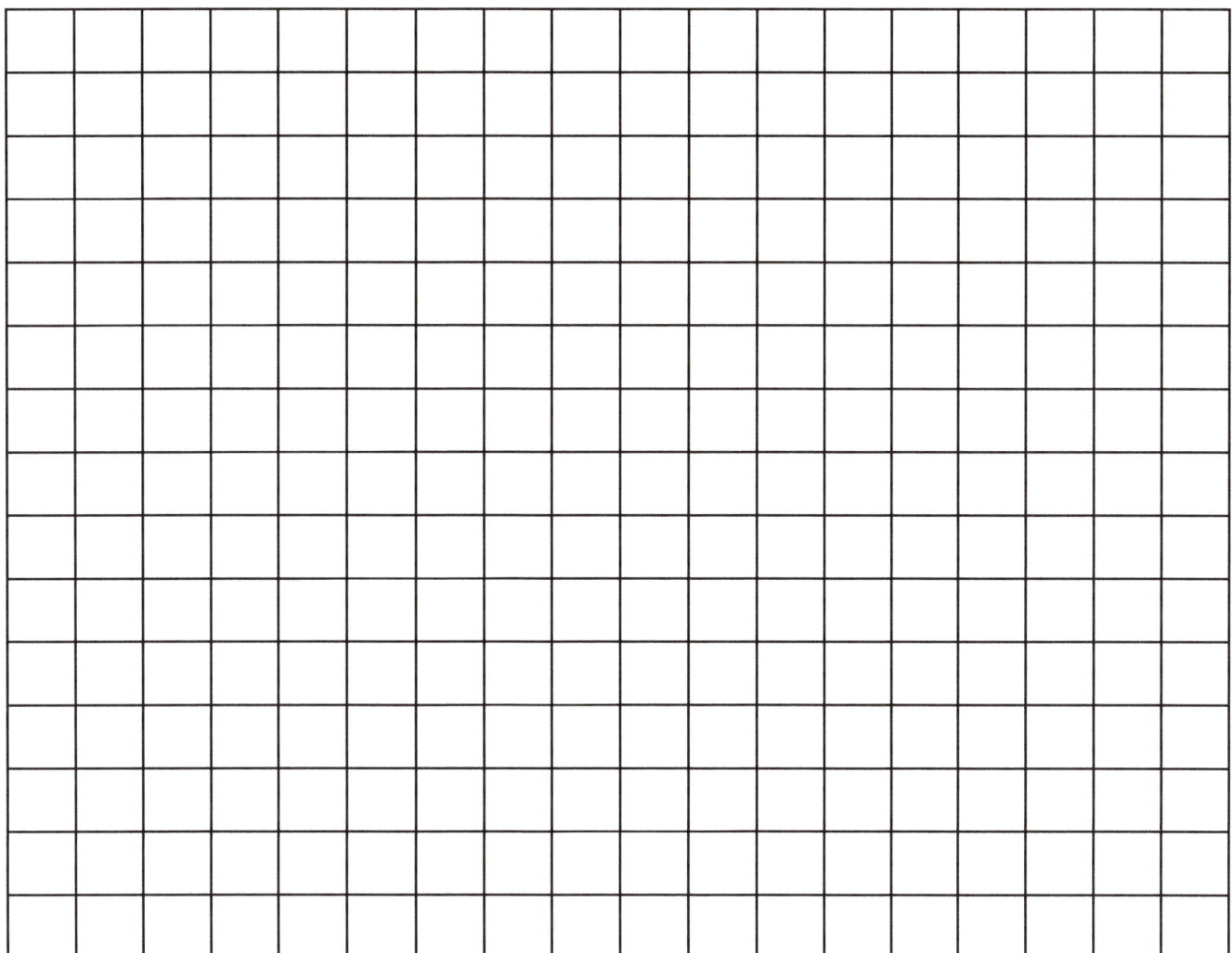

10. **Check the divisibility of all the given numbers.**

	Number	2	3	5	6	10
a.	648					
b.	720					
c.	1045					
d.	996					
e.	275					

Fractions

1. **Write an equivalent fraction for the given fractions.**

   a. $\dfrac{2}{7}$ = ☐   b. $\dfrac{3}{18}$ = ☐   c. $\dfrac{4}{9}$ = ☐

2. **Express the following mixed numbers as improper fractions.**

   a. $3\dfrac{1}{8}$ = ☐   b. $7\dfrac{6}{7}$ = ☐   c. $3\dfrac{9}{10}$ = ☐

3. **Express the following improper fractions as mixed numbers.**

   a. $\dfrac{12}{5}$ = ☐   b. $\dfrac{37}{7}$ = ☐   c. $\dfrac{78}{8}$ = ☐

4. **Reduce the fractions to their lowest term.**

   a. $\dfrac{66}{77}$ = ☐   b. $\dfrac{9}{48}$ = ☐   c. $\dfrac{21}{42}$ = ☐

5. **Solve the fractions and reduce them to the lowest term.**

   a. $\dfrac{5}{12} + \dfrac{4}{12}$

   _____

   b. $\dfrac{6}{15} - \dfrac{1}{15}$

   _____

   c. $\dfrac{3}{8} + \dfrac{3}{8}$

   _____

6. **Compare the fractions by finding the LCM of the denominators.**

   a. $\dfrac{4}{7}$ ☐ $\dfrac{2}{3}$
   b. $\dfrac{6}{11}$ ☐ $\dfrac{6}{13}$
   c. $\dfrac{1}{4}$ ☐ $\dfrac{2}{3}$

   d. $\dfrac{7}{10}$ ☐ $\dfrac{4}{5}$
   e. $\dfrac{8}{9}$ ☐ $\dfrac{2}{5}$
   f. $\dfrac{3}{8}$ ☐ $\dfrac{3}{10}$

7. **Fill in the blanks to make equivalent fractions.**

   a. $\dfrac{6}{13} = \dfrac{\square}{39}$
   b. $\dfrac{4}{32} = \dfrac{2}{\square}$
   c. $\dfrac{5}{8} = \dfrac{\square}{32}$

   d. $\dfrac{5}{11} = \dfrac{50}{\square}$
   e. $\dfrac{5}{65} = \dfrac{1}{\square}$
   f. $\dfrac{9}{30} = \dfrac{\square}{10}$

8. **Write the fractions in ascending order.**

   a. $\dfrac{1}{7}$, $\dfrac{2}{5}$, $\dfrac{3}{8}$

   _____

   b. $\dfrac{5}{6}$, $\dfrac{4}{5}$, $\dfrac{1}{8}$

   _____

9. **Write the fractions in descending order.**

   a. $\dfrac{1}{3}$, $\dfrac{2}{9}$, $\dfrac{5}{6}$

   _____

   b. $\dfrac{3}{8}$, $\dfrac{5}{6}$, $\dfrac{1}{4}$

   _____

10. Add the following fractions and find the sum.

a. $\frac{3}{7}$ and $\frac{5}{8}$ ☐   b. $\frac{2}{9}$ and $\frac{3}{4}$ ☐

c. $1\frac{4}{5}$ and $3\frac{2}{7}$ ☐   d. $2\frac{3}{8}$ and $5\frac{1}{6}$ ☐

11. Subtract the following fractions and find the difference.

a. $\frac{3}{8}$ from $\frac{4}{5}$ ☐   b. $\frac{2}{5}$ from $\frac{7}{10}$ ☐

c. $2\frac{1}{3}$ from $6\frac{5}{9}$ ☐   d. $1\frac{3}{4}$ from $3\frac{11}{12}$ ☐

12. Solve and simplify.

$2\frac{7}{10} + 1\frac{4}{5} - 4\frac{1}{2}$ ☐

13. Multiply and simplify.

a. $\frac{5}{8} \times 12$ ☐   b. $\frac{3}{7} \times 28$ ☐

c. $\frac{8}{7} \times \frac{1}{2}$ ☐   d. $\frac{4}{15} \times \frac{3}{8}$ ☐

e. $3\frac{1}{3} \times 2\frac{3}{5}$ ☐   f. $1\frac{5}{7} \times \frac{1}{3}$ ☐

14. Write the reciprocals for the following fractions.

a. $\frac{1}{9}$ ☐   b. $\frac{3}{7}$ ☐

c. $1\frac{6}{8}$ ☐   d. $4\frac{3}{5}$ ☐

15. Divide and simplify.

a. $6 \div \frac{1}{8}$ ☐   b. $\frac{14}{7} \div \frac{11}{12}$ ☐

c. $\frac{15}{8} \div \frac{22}{9}$ ☐   d. $3\frac{3}{5} \div 2\frac{1}{4}$ ☐

e. $6\frac{3}{5} \div 1\frac{4}{7}$ ☐   f. $16 \div 2\frac{4}{5}$ ☐

16. Fill in the blanks with the correct answer.

a. A fraction is an equal part of a _____.

b. _____ fractions have different denominators whereas _____ fractions have the same denominators.

c. A _____ fraction is a combination of a whole number and a proper fraction.

d. Reciprocal of a fraction is also called the _____.

e. Any fraction multiplied by 0 gives _____ as a product.

17. Choose the correct answer for following questions.

a. The reciprocal of fraction $1\frac{11}{7}$ is _____.

   (i) $2\frac{7}{4}$ (ii) $\frac{7}{18}$ (iii) $\frac{18}{7}$

b. The LCM of the denominators of $\frac{1}{3}$, $\frac{4}{8}$ and $\frac{5}{6}$ is _____.

   (i) 18   (ii) 48   (iii) 24

c. An equivalent fraction of $\frac{6}{16}$ with 40 as the denominator.

   (i) $\frac{12}{40}$ (ii) $\frac{14}{40}$ (iii) $\frac{3}{8}$

d. An equivalent fraction of $\frac{3}{8}$ with 9 as the numerator.

   (i) $\frac{3}{8}$ (ii) $\frac{3}{7}$ (iii) $\frac{3}{9}$

e. The LCM of the denominators of $\frac{2}{7}$, $\frac{1}{4}$ and $\frac{14}{3}$ is _____.

   (i) 21   (ii) 84   (iii) 28

18. Solve the given word problems.

a. Suman has 18 bags of fruits each weighing $1\frac{3}{4}$ kg. If she delivers 2 bags to a customer, how much weight is she carrying now?

b. A tailor needs $4\frac{3}{4}$ m of cloth for making shirts and $8\frac{1}{4}$ m cloth for making trousers for a dance group. How much cloth does he need in all?

c. $\frac{1}{6}$ Students of a class opted for English, $\frac{2}{3}$ opted for French and the rest opted for German as second language. If there are 78 students in the class, how many will learn German?

d. A birthday cake was divided into equal slices. If $\frac{5}{8}$ of the cake was consumed and 24 slices were left, how many slices were consumed?

e. A carton weighing $12\frac{2}{9}$ kg contains 11 books of equal size. Find the weight of 7 such books?

f. A lady drinks $4\frac{3}{5}$ l of water in the first half of the day and $2\frac{2}{5}$ l of water in the second half. How much quantity of water (in l) does she drink in a day?

g. There are 75 fruits in a basket each weighing $\frac{2}{15}$ kg. What will be the total weight of the basket if 30 more such fruits are added to it?

Working Space

Decimals

A. Write the following decimals in words.

1. 0.43 _____

2. 56.8 _____

3. 109.74 _____

4. 3.25 _____

5. 0.842 _____

6. 7.059 _____

7. 125.286 _____

8. 10.001 _____

B. Convert the following fractions into decimals.

1. $\frac{6}{10}$ = _____   2. $\frac{24}{10}$ = _____

3. $\frac{1}{100}$ = _____   4. $\frac{36}{100}$ = _____

5. $\frac{42}{1000}$ = _____   6. $\frac{17}{10}$ = _____

7. $\frac{364}{1000}$ = _____   8. $\frac{8}{1000}$ = _____

C. **Write the place value of the underlined digit in each of the following decimals.**

1. 3<u>6</u>.04 _____
2. 32.14<u>8</u> _____
3. 19.<u>5</u>7 _____
4. 705.8<u>6</u>6 _____
5. <u>8</u>5.921 _____
6. 64.00<u>7</u> _____
7. 9.<u>9</u>9 _____
8. 46.0<u>8</u>2 _____

D. **Expand the following decimal numbers in two different ways.**

	Decimal number	Expanded decimal form	Expanded fractional form
1.	13.84	10 + 3 + 0.8 + 0.04	10 + 3 + $\frac{8}{10}$ + $\frac{4}{100}$
2.	7.727		
3.	35.08		
4.	81.004		
5.	462.199		
6.	6.48		

E. **Arrange the following numbers in the ascending order.**

1. 0.36, 1.47, 0.192, 2.5, 0.1, 3.55

   _____

2. 2.37, 2.73, 2.037, 2.073, 2.733, 2.3

   _____

3. 11.1, 12.2, 21.1, 13.112, 11.121, 2.113

   _____

F. Arrange the following numbers in the descending order.

1. 4.562, 2.465, 624.5, 0.462, 4.25, 56.24

   _____

2. 21.004, 21.04, 12.004, 12.04, 12.4, 21.4

   _____

3. 0.34, 0.3, 0.345, 2.345, 23.45, 1.345

   _____

G. Arrange the numbers in vertical columns and solve.

1. 12.846 + 10.729	2. 67.049 − 42.425
3. 734.012 − 429.008	4. 49.456 + 25.92
5. 2.4 × 1.6	6. 10.12 × 3.4
7. 37.800 ÷ 100	8. 286.45 ÷ 5

H. Solve the following word problems.

1. A lady bought bananas worth $42.75 and oranges worth $38.62. If she gives $90 to the fruitseller, how much money will she get back?

2. A milkman sells 52.35 l milk in the morning and 36.42 l milk in the evening. How much milk does he sell in a day?

3. A company manufactures juice bottles of capacity 1.25 l. If the company sold 364 bottles of juice in a week, how much quantity of juice was sold by the company in 2 weeks?

4. A tailor used 35.58 m cloth to make 6 dresses. If each dress was made using equal lengths of cloth, how much cloth was used to make one dress?

5. In a competition, team 1 scored 135.26 points, team 2 scored 156.35 points and team 3 scored 116.57 points. By how many points did the winning team win compared to the team that came third in the competition?

6. A water tank of capacity 465.3 l was used to fill 11 containers of equal size. How much water will be there in 5 such containers?

7. The weight of a sack of flour was 265.200 kg. Due to negligence, 96.520 kg flour spread outside. How much flour is left in the sack?

8. The length of a scarf is 1.75 m. What will be the length of 15 such scarves together?

Patterns and Symmetry

1. Draw horizontal or vertical lines of symmetry for the following flat shapes.

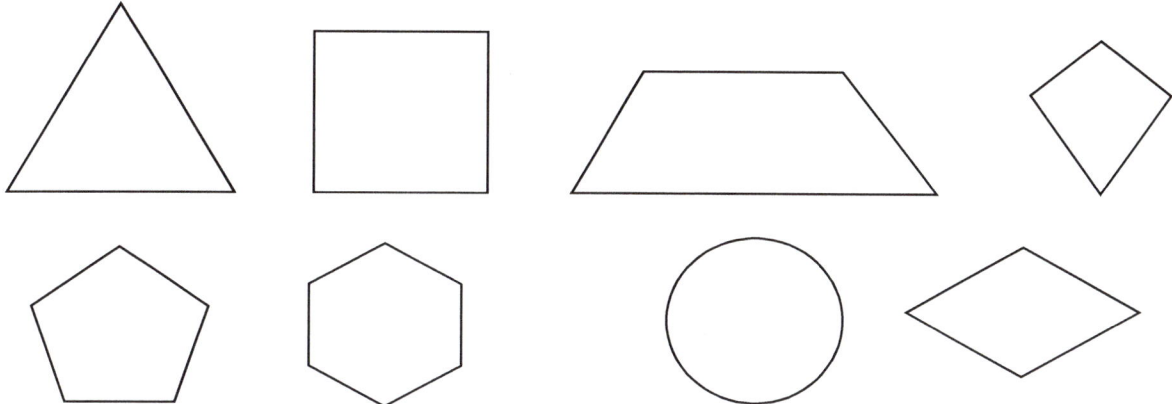

2. Draw four capital letters of the English alphabet which have two or more lines of symmetry.

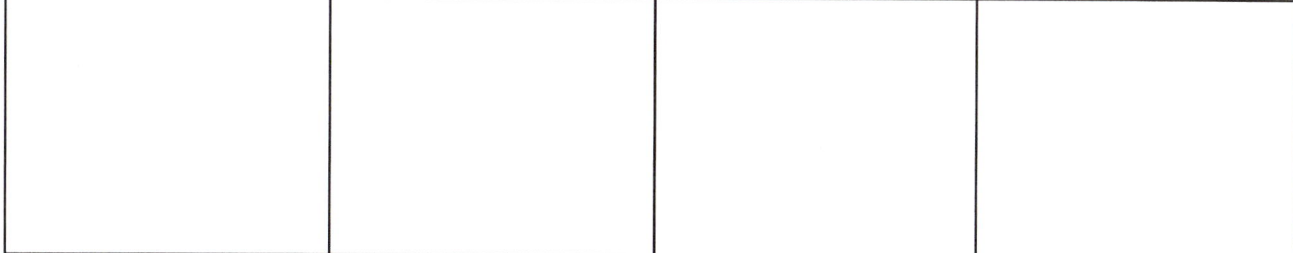

3. Complete the following symmetrical shapes along the given line of symmetry.

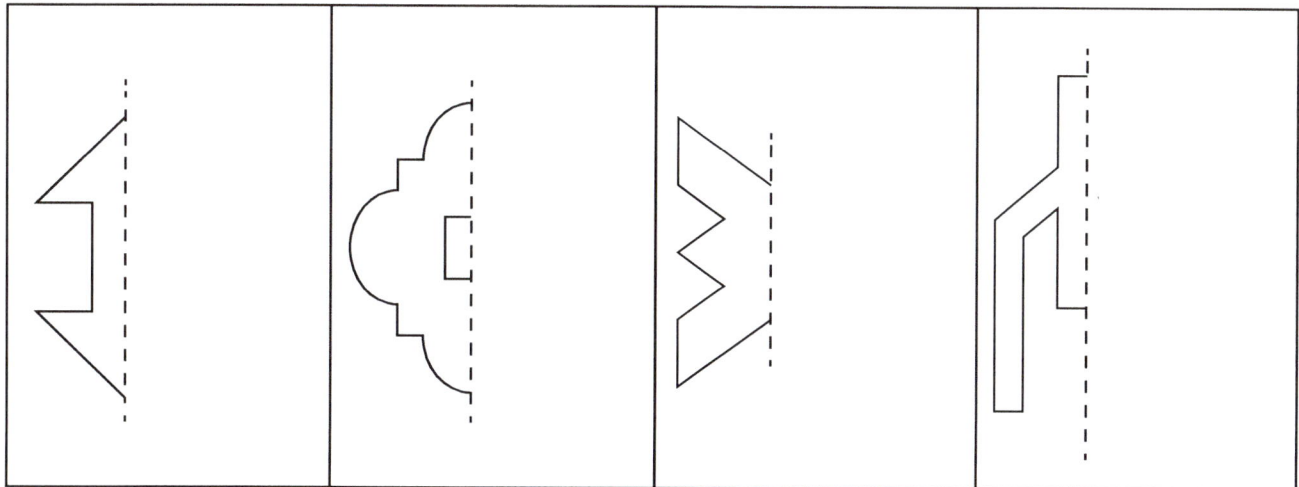

4. Flip the following shapes across the given line.

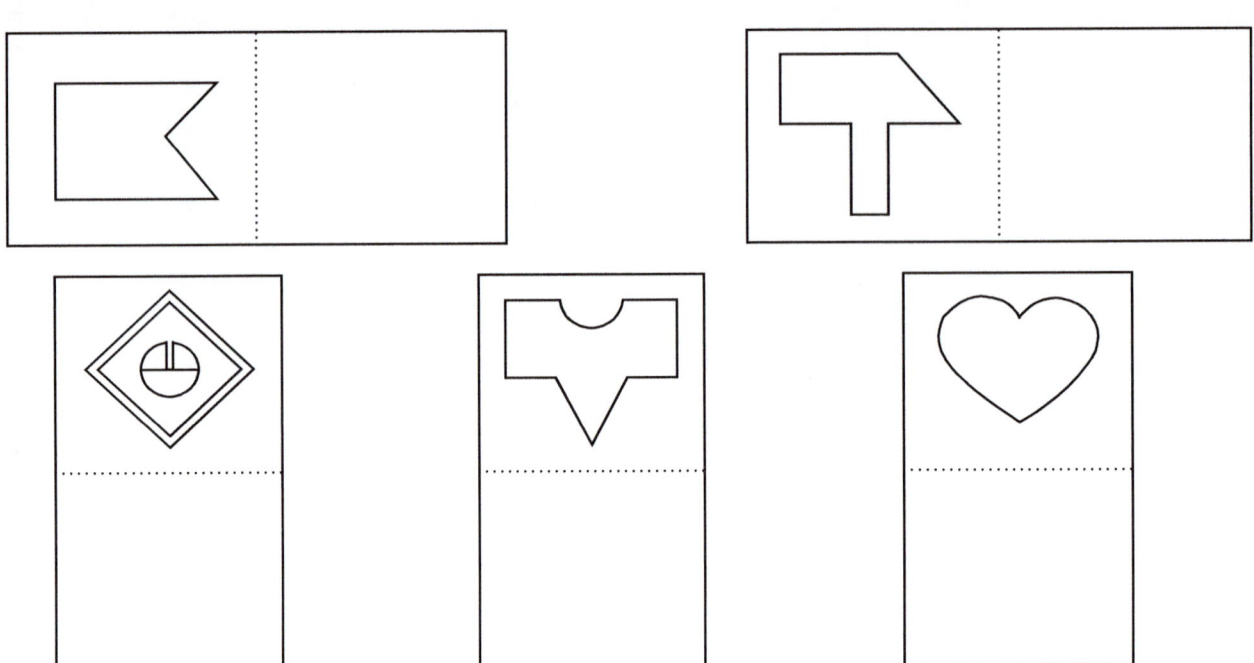

5. Draw two letters from the English alphabet and two numbers which look the same after being flipped vertically.

Letter _____	Letter _____	Number _____	Number _____

6. Turn the shapes and complete the table.

Shape	$\frac{1}{4}$ Turn	$\frac{1}{2}$ Turn	$\frac{3}{4}$ Turn
(a) ⬆			
(b) ⬠			
(c) ▶			

7. **Name six natural objects with patterns in them.**

a. _____ b. _____ c. _____

d. _____ e. _____ f. _____

8. **Observe the patterns on leaves, flowers, animals and other natural objects. Draw two patterns in the given space and colour them.**

(a)

(b)

9. **Complete the following number patterns.**

a. 7, 12, 17, 22, _____, _____, _____, _____.

b. 1, 2, 4, 8, 16, _____, _____, _____, _____.

c. 0, 1, 3, 6, 10, _____, _____, _____, _____.

d. 6, 12, 18, 24, _____, _____, _____, _____.

e. 1, 3, 5, 7, 9, _____, _____, _____, _____.

10. **Study the pattern and write the next terms.**

(a)
$1 \times 1 = 1$
$11 \times 11 = 1\ 2\ 1$
$111 \times 111 = 1\ 2\ 3\ 2\ 1$
____ × ____ = ____
____ × ____ = ____
____ × ____ = ____

(b)
$3 \times 37{,}037 = 1{,}11{,}111$
$6 \times 37{,}037 = 2{,}22{,}222$
$9 \times 37{,}037 = 3{,}33{,}333$
____ × ____ = _____
____ × ____ = _____
____ × ____ = _____

Geometry

1. Look at the figure given below and name the following.

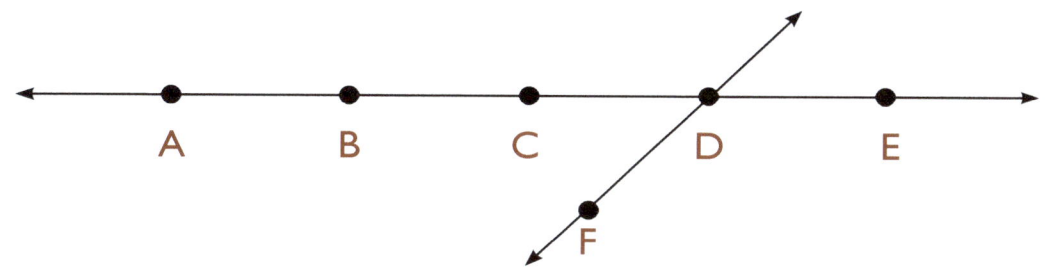

a. 3 line segments _____ , _____ , _____

b. 3 rays _____ , _____ , _____

c. 2 lines _____ , _____

d. 4 points _____ , _____ , _____ , _____

e. 2 angles _____ , _____

2. See the figure and follow the steps to complete it.

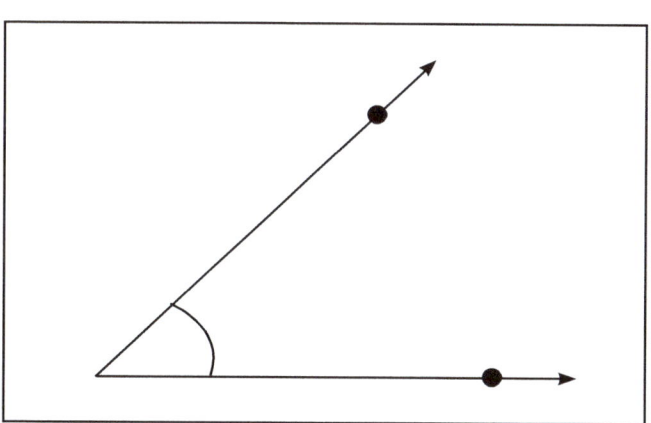

1. Draw 3 points in the interior of the angles.

2. Draw two points in the exterior of the angle.

3. Label the angle and the points.

4. Name the arms of the angle.

5. Name the angle. _____

6. Name the vertex of the angle. _____

3. **Draw angles of the given measurements and label them.**

a. ∠PSR = 50°	b. ∠MON = 135°

4. **Measure the following angles using a protractor and classify them on the basis of their measurements.**

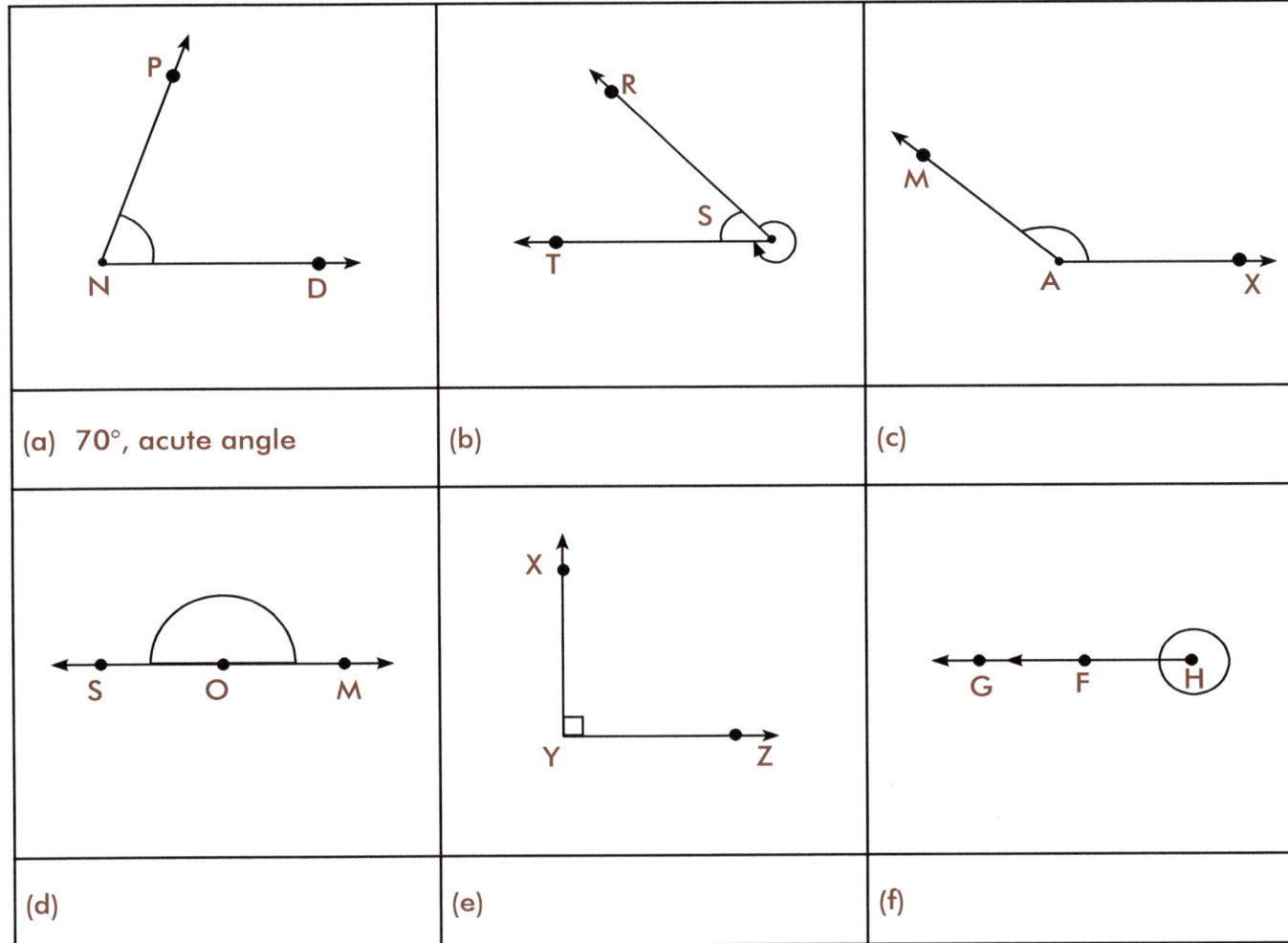

(a) 70°, acute angle (b) (c)

(d) (e) (f)

34

5. **Observe the given figure carefully and answer the following.**

   a. Name three collinear points. _____

   b. Name a straight angle. _____

   c. Name three non-collinear points. _____

   d. Name a right angle. _____

   e. ∠NSR = _____

   f. Name an obtuse angle. _____

   g. Name all the acute angles. _____

   h. Name the arms of ∠PSR. _____

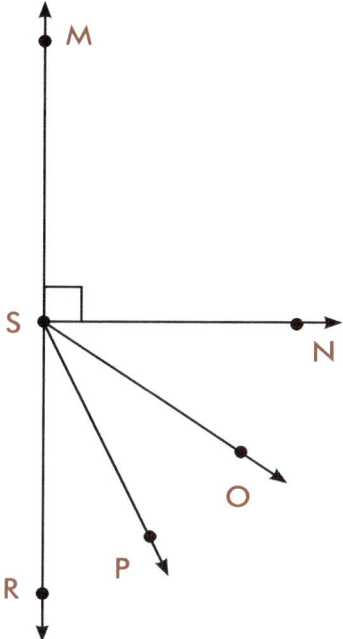

6. **Identify whether the following letters have parallel lines intersecting lines, or perpendicular lines.**

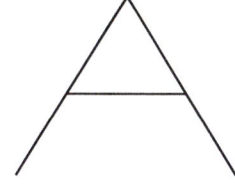

a. _____

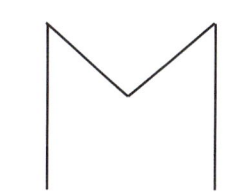

b. _____

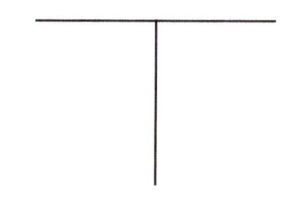

c. _____

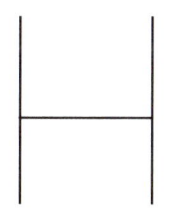

d. _____

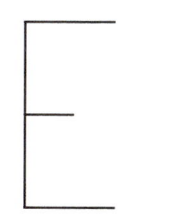

e. _____

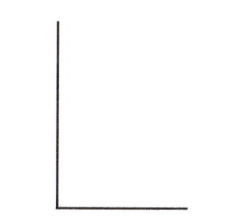

f. _____

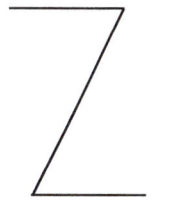

g. _____

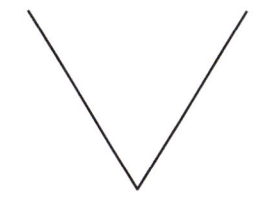

h. _____

i. _____

7. Draw three digits from 0 to 9 which have intersecting lines in them.

8. Use a ruler and draw the following lines.

   a. PQ ⊥ RS

   b. BN ‖ AD

9. Classify the triangles on the basis of the given measurements.

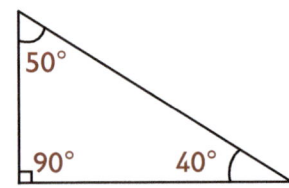 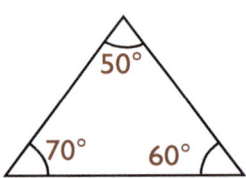 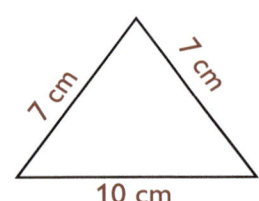

a. _____   b. _____   c. _____

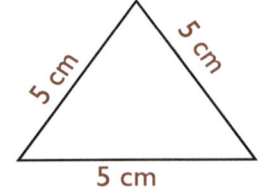 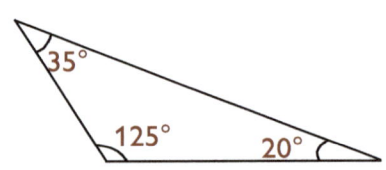 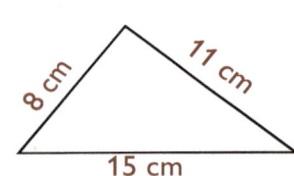

d. _____   e. _____   f. _____

10. Name the following regular polygons.

(a)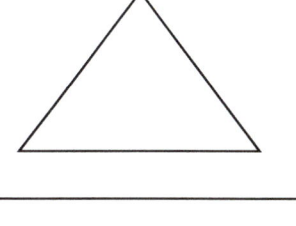

(b)

(c)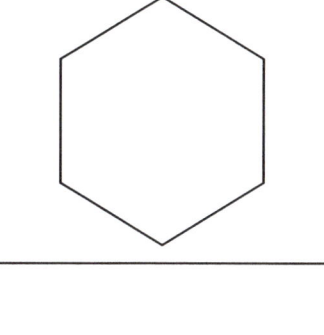

(d)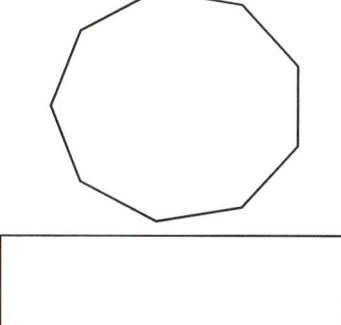

(e)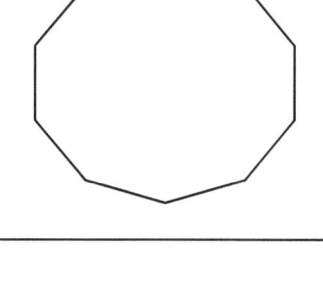

(f)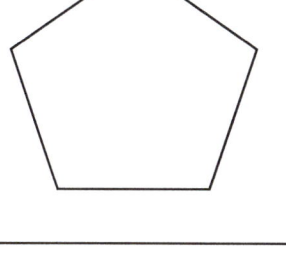

(g)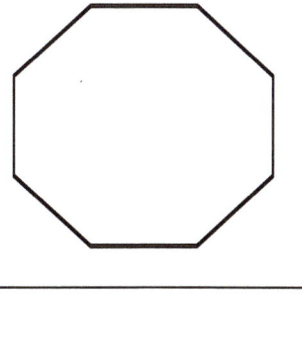

(h)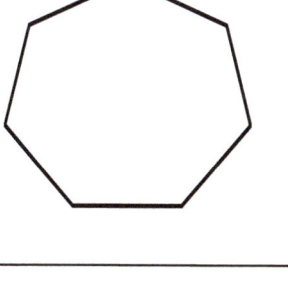

11. Draw a circle of radius 5 cm with the help of a compass in the space given below. Mark the following on it and name them.

a. Centre _____

b. A diameter _____

c. A radius _____

d. A chord _____

e. An arc _____

f. 2 points on the circle _____

12. Write Yes for the statements which can be possible and No for the ones which are not possible.

a. An isosceles triangle with a right angle. ☐

b. An arc equal to the length of a semi-circle. ☐

c. Two parallel lines which meet at a point X. ☐

d. A triangle with three acute angles. ☐

e. A triangle with sides 9 cm, 5 cm and 3 cm. ☐

f. A chord which is equal to the diameter of the circle. ☐

g. Three collinear points joined to make a triangle. ☐

h. A triangle with angles 110°, 40° and 30°. ☐

i. A circle can be called a polygon. ☐

13. Fill in the blanks.

a. The lines passing through the same point are called _____.

b. Three or more points which lie in a straight line are called _____.

c. The other name for ∠ABX is _____.

d. We can use a _____ to measure an angle.

e. An angle whose measure is 90° is called a _____.

f. A reflex angle measures more than _____ but less than _____.

g. The measurement of a complete angle is _____.

h. The opposite edges of a ruler are an example of _____ line.

i. The symbol for perpendicular lines is _____ and that of parallel lines is _____.

j. The letter Y of the English alphabet is an example of _____ lines.

k. A triangle with all sides of equal length is called an _____.

l. The sum of all three angles of a triangle is always _____.

14. Define the following terms in one sentence.

a. Ray : _____

b. Plane : _____

c. Polygon : _____

d. Circle : _____

e. Quadrilateral : _____

f. Circumference : _____

g. Semicircle : _____

Perimeter

A. Find the perimeter of the following.

1.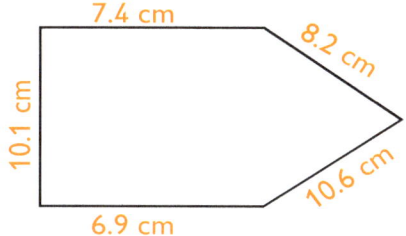

   Perimeter = _____ cm

2.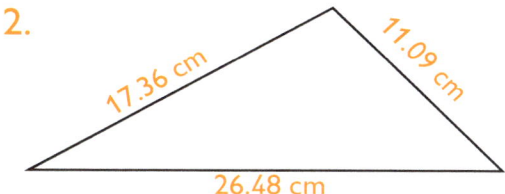

   Perimeter = _____ cm

3.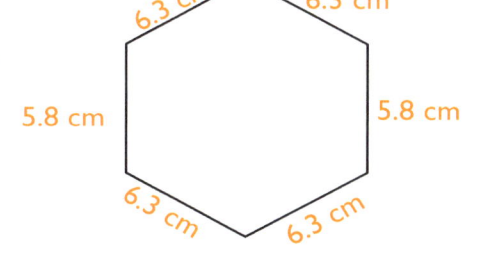

   Perimeter = _____ cm

4.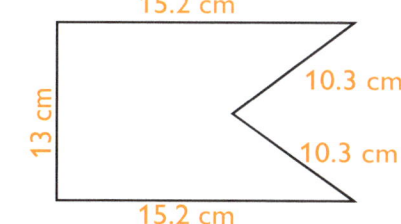

   Perimeter = _____ cm

B. Find the perimeter of the shapes using the given data.

1. The length of a rectangle is 4.5 cm and breadth is 6 cm. _____

2. The length of a rectangle is 12.8 m and breadth is 6.7 m. _____

3. The sides of a triangle are 10 cm, 6.5 cm and 8.7 cm. _____

4. The side of a square is 26.4 m. _____

5. The side of a square is 19 cm. _____

6. The sides of a triangle are 4.5 cm, 6.8 cm and 8.7 cm. _____

7. The length and breadth of a rectangle are 15.4 cm and 8.6 cm respectively. _____

8. The side of a square is 15.7 cm. _____

C.   Find the answers of the given word problems.

1. What is the perimeter of an equivalent triangle with side 17 cm? _____

2. Mayank walks around a rectangular park with sides 7.8 cm and 3.7 cm. If he takes three rounds of the park, how much did he walk in all?

3. The perimeter of a square table is 44 m. What is the length of its side? _____

4. A tailor puts a lace around a rectangular carpet with sides 2.5 m and 4.5 m. How much lace was used by him? _____

5. A square table cloth was cut into two equal halves. If its side was 28 cm, what is the perimeter of each half? _____

6. Two adjacent sides of an isosceles triangle are 3.5 cm in length and the third side is 6 cm. What is the perimeter of the triangle? _____

7. Measure the length of your desk and write it in the following units:
   _____ mm , _____ cm , _____ m

8. The perimeter of a square banner is 36 m. What length of iron rod is required to build a frame for the banner? _____

9. Find the perimeter of a television screen with length 24 cm and breadth 18 cm. _____

10. What length of square fence will be required to put around a building with sides 37.5 metres? _____

Metric Measurements

A. Fill in the blanks given below.

1. The standard unit for measuring length is _____.

2. The standard unit for measuring weight is _____.

3. The standard unit for measuring capacity is _____.

4. 1 km = _____ m.

5. 1 l = _____ ml.

6. 1 m = _____ cm.

7. 1 kg = _____ g.

8. 1 cm = _____ mm.

9. 1 g = _____ mg.

B. Convert the following into the given units.

1. 4 kg 53 g = _____ g.

2. 12 km 182 m = _____ m.

3. 7 cm 8 mm = _____ mm.

4. 5 l = _____ ml.

5. 3 l 540 ml = _____ ml.

6. 8620 mm = _____ cm.

7. 9 m 78 cm = _____ cm.

8. 17260 m = _____ km _____ m.

9. 78690 g = _____ kg _____ g.

10. 6200 ml = _____ l _____ ml.

11. 2890 cm = _____ m _____ cm.

12. 13 l 784 ml = _____ ml.

C. Write the proper unit for measuring each of the following.

1. The capacity of a bottle of water.   _____

2. The weight of apples at your home.   _____

3. The distance from your school to your house. _____

4. The length of your pencil.   _____

5. The weight of your lunch box.   _____

D. Solve the following.

a) 15 kg 380 g + 7 kg 642 g

b) 18 km – 3 km 428 m

c) 62 l 250 ml − 41 l 187 ml

d) 30 m − 1462 cm

E. Solve the following word problems.

1. The height of two trees is 7 m 18 cm and 3 m 47 cm respectively. What is the difference in the heights of the two trees?

   Answer: _____

2. Rohan is carrying 18 bags. Each bag weights 750 grams. What is the total weight that he is carrying?

   Answer: _____

3. A shopkeeper sold two pieces of cloth of lengths 7648 cm and 4329 cm respectively. Find the total length of the cloth sold by him.

   Answer: _____

Answers

Large Numbers

2. a. Thirty eight lakh forty two thousand nine hundred fifty
   b. One crore four lakh thirty six thousand eight
   c. Eighty six lakh fifty four thousand thirty seven
   d. Two crore fifty nine lakh eighty thousand eight hundred fifty six
   e. Seven crore four lakh thirteen thousand eight hundred six

3. a. 200700 b. 80008
   c. 10000020 d. 3002000

4. a. 6600000 b. 29998000
   c. 899998 d. 79950

5. a. 6004713 b. 37500801
   c. 2064569 d. 10853087
   e. 1529920

6. a. 30000000 + 4000000 + 900000 + 8000 + 400 + 60 + 2
   b. 500000000 + 800000 + 20000 + 60 + 7
   c. 20000000 + 7000000 + 900000 + 80000 + 4000 + 600
   d. 8000000 + 600000 + 8000 + 50 + 9
   e. 70000000 + 3000000 + 600000 + 40000 + 700 + 8

7. a. 3,29,188   3,29,190   b. 76,99,998   77,00,000
   c. 4,99,99,999   5,00,00,001   d. 36,29,079   36,29,081
   e. 72,46,89,998   72,46,90,000

8. a. <   b. =   c. <   d. <
   e. <   f. <   g. >   h. <

9. a. 8843310, 1033488   b. 98753220, 20235789
   c. 98765431, 13456789   d. 98766420, 20466789
   e. 98753210, 10235789   f. 87421100, 10012478

10. a. 3256728, 3392647, 3642897, 3682497, 3824926
    b. 60052947, 60198527, 61098572, 65284272, 69084217

11. a. 8475600, 8472650, 8472560, 8465270, 8427650
    b. 14892700, 14297600, 14286700, 14209670, 14205267

12. a. 10,99,99,999   b. 9,99,999
    c. 99,89,999   d. 5,00,00,000
    e. 19,99,999   f. 9,99,99,998
    g. 10,001   h. 1,00,00,000

13. a. 6,74,000   b. 75,01,000   c. 28,94,000
    d. 16,42,000   e. 28,69,000   f. 2,37,01,000

14. a. 18,84,100   b. 37,64,600   c. 80,04,300
    d. 6,80,000   e. 25,08,000   f. 2,64,500

15. a. 29,80,000   b. 6,19,40,000   c. 64,70,000
    d. 30,00,000   e. 23,30,000   f. 71,50,000

16. a. Six lakh forty three thousand
    b. Three lakh four thousand
    c. Eighty three thousand
    d. Six lakh fifteen thousand

17. a. 75   b. 202   c. 1555
    d. 1212   e. 965   f. 119
    g. 157   h. 538   i. 2054

18. a. MDCCXX   b. DCCC   c. MMXVII
    d. DLXVIII   e. MCX   f. CCLIII

19. g. CMXLVII   h. CDIV   i. MDCXVI
    b. CCCLXVI   c. DCCXX   d. XXVI
    e. CMXCIX   f. M   g. CXXXV
    h. II, III, V, VII, XI   j. DXCVIII
    k. CMXCIX

Arithmetic Operations

1. a. 8,99,332   b. 28,91,102
   c. 59,56,450   d. 1,98,433
   e. 76,78,796   f. 5,15,481

2. a. 283468 + 492708 = 776176
   b. 8007008 − 3264705 = 4742303

3. a. 27,87,836   b. 61,07,868   c. 51,95,796
   d. 1   e. 83,32,298   f. 15,06,651
   g. 22,17,411   h. 59,93,747

4. a. 21,593   b. 39,63,472   c. $58,37,800
   d. 78,21,120 kg

5. a. 10,28,643   b. 9,88,898   c. 12,34,791
   d. 11,48,271   e. 12,23,901   f. 18,68,931
   g. 18,95,390

6. a. 1,29,60,500   b. 49,43,632   c. 3294
   d. 71600

7. a. 6,42,800   b. 3,20,50,000   c. 1,52,680
   d. 36,21,360   e. 600   f. 900
   g. 67,290   h. 10   i. 2,37,650
   j. 8,426

8. a. 1131438 toys   b. 559260 stamps, 0 stamps left
   c. 89670 pages   d. 65730 people

9. a. 277641   b. 344980

10. a. 432000   b. 451000   c. 58000
    d. 845000   e. 5478000

11. a. 5,40,000 leaves   b. 35000 stamps
    c. 9000000 books

12. a. 1999999   b. 1   c. 9999000
    d. 10000   e. 0   f. 56700
    g. 674, 40

13. a. 9, 8   b. 1, 1   c. 3, 4
    d. 4   e. 6   f. 3, 3, 3
    g. 5, 9, 8

Factors and Multiples

1. a. 1   b. factors
   c. multiples   d. two
   e. composite   f. HCF, LCM
   g. Highest Common Factor, Lowest Common Multiple
   h. twin primes

2. a. 1, 2, 4, 8, 16, 32   b. 1, 3, 5, 15
   c. 1, 2, 4, 5, 8, 10, 20, 40   d. 1, 2, 4, 7, 14, 28
   e. 1, 2, 3, 6, 11, 22, 33, 66   f. 1, 2, 7, 14

3. a. 8, 16, 24   b. 15, 30, 45   c. 5, 10, 15
   d. 10, 20, 30   e. 22, 44, 66   f. 11, 22, 33
4. 23, 29, 31, 37, 41, 43, 47, 53, 59
5. 3 and 5, 5 and 7, 11 and 13, 17 and 19, 29 and 31, 41 and 43, 59 and 61, 71 and 73
6. a. $72 = 2 \times 2 \times 2 \times 3 \times 3$
   b. $150 = 2 \times 3 \times 5 \times 5$
   c. $176 = 2 \times 2 \times 2 \times 2 \times 11$
   d. $108 = 2 \times 2 \times 3 \times 3 \times 3$
7. a. LCM = 42   b. LCM = 24
8. a. LCM = 150   b. 45
   c. 23   d. HCF=3, LCM=135
   e. 385   f. 12

Fractions

1. a. $\frac{4}{14}$ b. $\frac{1}{6}$ c. $\frac{8}{18}$
2. a. $\frac{25}{8}$ b. $\frac{55}{7}$ c. $\frac{39}{10}$
3. a. $2\frac{2}{5}$ b. $5\frac{2}{7}$ c. $9\frac{6}{8}$
4. a. $\frac{6}{7}$ b. $\frac{3}{16}$ c. $\frac{1}{2}$
5. a. $\frac{3}{4}$ b. $\frac{1}{3}$ c. $\frac{3}{4}$
6. a. <   b. >   c. <   d. <
   e. >   f. >
7. a. 18   b. 16   c. 20
   d. 110   e. 13   f. 3
8. a. $\frac{1}{7}, \frac{3}{8}, \frac{2}{5}$ b. $\frac{1}{8}, \frac{4}{5}, \frac{5}{6}$
9. a. $\frac{5}{6}, \frac{1}{3}, \frac{2}{9}$ b. $\frac{5}{6}, \frac{3}{8}, \frac{1}{4}$
10. a. $\frac{59}{56}$ b. $\frac{35}{36}$ c. $\frac{178}{35}$ d. $\frac{181}{24}$
11. a. $\frac{17}{40}$ b. $\frac{3}{10}$ c. $\frac{38}{9}$ d. $\frac{13}{6}$
12. 0
13. a. $7\frac{1}{2}$ b. 12   c. $\frac{4}{7}$
    d. $\frac{1}{10}$ e. $8\frac{2}{3}$ f. $\frac{4}{7}$
14. a. $\frac{9}{1}$ b. $\frac{7}{3}$ c. $\frac{8}{14}$ d. $\frac{5}{23}$
15. a. 48   b. $\frac{24}{11}$ c. $\frac{135}{176}$
    d. $\frac{8}{5}$ e. $\frac{21}{5}$ f. $\frac{40}{7}$
16. a. whole   b. unlike, like
    c. mixed   d. multiplicative inverse
    e. 0
17. a. (ii)   b. (iii)   c. (iii)
    d. (i)   e. (ii)
18. a. 28 kg   b. 13 m   c. 13
    d. 13   d. 40 slices   e. $7\frac{7}{9}$ kg
    f. 7 l   g. 14 kg

Decimals

A. 1. Zero point four three
   2. Fifty six point eight
   3. One hundred nine point seven four
   4. Three point two five
   5. Zero point eight four two
   6. Seven point zero five nine
   7. One hundred twenty five point two eight six
   8. Ten point zero zero one
B. 1. 0.6   2. 2.4   3. 0.01
   4. 0.36   5. 0.042   6. 1.7
   7. 0.364   8. 0.008
C. 1. 6 ones   2. 8 thousandths
   3. 5 tenths   4. 6 hundredths
   5. 8 tens   6. 7 thousandths
   7. 9 tenths   8. 8 hundredths
D. 1. $10 + 3 + 0.8 + 0.04$, $10 + 3 + \frac{8}{10} + \frac{4}{100}$
   2. $7 + 0.7 + 0.02 + 0.007$, $7 + \frac{7}{10} + \frac{2}{100} + \frac{7}{1000}$
   3. $30 + 5 + 0.08$, $30 + 5 + \frac{8}{100}$
   4. $80 + 1 + 0.004$, $80 + 1 + \frac{4}{1000}$
   5. $400 + 60 + 2 + 0.1 + 0.09 + 0.009$, $400 + 60 + 2 + \frac{1}{10} + \frac{9}{100} + \frac{9}{1000}$
   6. $6 + 0.4 + 0.08$, $6 + \frac{4}{10} + \frac{8}{100}$
E. 1. 0.1, 0.192, 0.36, 1.47, 2.5, 3.55
   2. 2.037, 2.073, 2.3, 2.37, 2.73, 2.733
   3. 2.113, 11.1, 11.121, 12.2, 13.112, 21.1
F. 1. 624.5, 56.24, 4.562, 4.25, 2.465, 0.462
   2. 21.4, 21.04, 21.004, 12.4, 12.04, 12.004
   3. 23.45, 2.345, 1.345, 0.345, 0.34, 0.3
G. 1. 23.575   2. 24.624   3. 305.004
   4. 75.376   5. 3.84   6. 34.408
   7. 0.378   8. 57.29
H. 1. $8.63   2. 88.77 l   3. 910 l
   4. 5.93 m   5. 39.78 points   6. 211.5 l
   7. 168.68 kg   8. 26.25 m

Patterns and Symmetry

9. a. 27, 32, 37, 42   b. 32, 64, 128, 256
   c. 15, 21, 28, 36   d. 30, 36, 42, 48
   e. 11, 13, 15, 17
10. a. $1111 \times 1111 = 1234321$
    $11111 \times 11111 = 123454321$
    $111111 \times 111111 = 12345654321$
    b. $12 \times 37037 = 4,44,444$
    $15 \times 37037 = 5,55,555$
    $18 \times 37037 = 6,66,666$

Geometry

1. a. $\overline{CD}$, $\overline{DB}$, $\overline{BC}$ b. $\vec{BA}$, $\vec{BE}$, $\vec{DE}$
   c. $\overleftrightarrow{AE}$, $\overleftrightarrow{DF}$ d. B, C, D, E, A
   e. ∠FDC, ∠FDE

5. a. R, S, M b. ∠MSR c. N, P, M
   d. ∠MSN, ∠RSN e. 90° f. ∠MSP, ∠MSO
   g. ∠RSP, ∠PSO, ∠RSO, ∠NSO, ∠NSP h. PS, SR

6. a. Intersecting lines
   b. Intersecting lines, Parallel lines
   c. Perpendicular lines
   d. Perpendicular lines, Parallel lines
   e. Perpendicular lines, Parallel lines
   f. Perpendicular lines
   g. Intersecting lines
   h. Intersecting lines
   i. Perpendicular lines, Intersecting lines

7. 4, 5, 7,

9. a. Right angled triangle
   b. Acute angled triangle
   c. Isosceles triangle
   d. Equilateral triangle
   e. Obtuse angled triangle
   f. Scalene triangle

10. a. Triangle b. Square
    c. Hexagon d. Nonagon
    e. Decagon f. Pentagon
    g. Octagon h. Septagon

12. a. Yes b. Yes c. No
    d. Yes e. No f. Yes
    g. No h. Yes i. No

13. a. concurrent lines b. collinear points
    c. ∠B d. protractor
    e. right angle f. 180°, 360°
    g. 360° h. parallel
    i. ⊥, ∥ j. intersecting
    k. equilateral triangle
    l. 180°

Perimeter

A. 1. 43.2 cm 2. 54.93 cm 3. 36.8 cm
   4. 64 cm

B. 1. 21 cm 2. 39 m 3. 25.2 cm
   4. 105.6 m 5. 76 cm 6. 20 cm
   7. 48 cm 8. 62.8 cm

C. 1. 51 cm 2. 69 cm 3. 11 m
   4. 14 m 5. 56 cm 6. 13 cm
   8. 9 m 9. 84 cm 10. 150 m

Metric Measurements

A. 1. m (metre) 2. kg (kilogram) 3. l (litre)
   4. 1000 5. 1000 6. 100
   7. 1000 8. 10 9. 1000

B. 1. 4053 2. 12182 3. 78
   4. 5000 5. 3540 6. 862
   7. 978 8. 17, 260 9. 78, 690
   10. 6, 200 11. 28, 90 12. 13784

C. 1. l 2. kg 3. km
   4. cm 5. g

D. a. 23 kg 22 g b. 14 km 572 m
   c. 21 l 63 ml d. 15 m 38 cm

E. 1. 3 m 71 cm 2. 13 kg 500 g 3. 119 m 77 cm

www.ingramcontent.com/pod-product-compliance
Lightning Source LLC
Chambersburg PA
CBHW040056160426
43192CB00002B/86